HAL•LEONARD
GUITAR PLAY-ALONG

REGGAE

VOL. 89

ISBN 978-1-4234-5195-2

HAL•LEONARD®
CORPORATION

7777 W. BLUEMOUND RD. P.O. BOX 13819 MILWAUKEE, WI 53213

For all works contained herein:
Unauthorized copying, arranging, adapting, recording, Internet posting, public performance,
or other distribution of the printed or recorded music in this publication is an infringement of copyright.
Infringers are liable under the law.

Visit Hal Leonard Online at
www.halleonard.com

CONTENTS

I Shot the Sheriff

Words and Music by Bob Marley

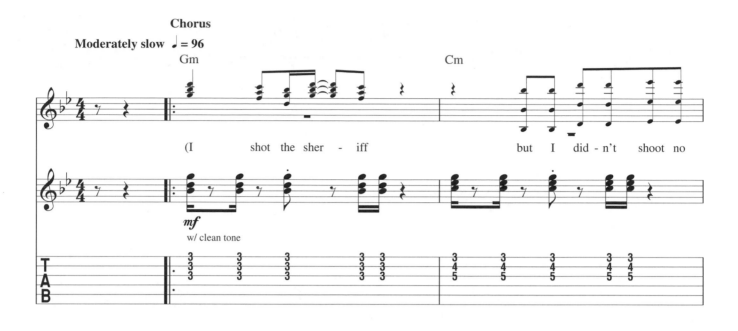

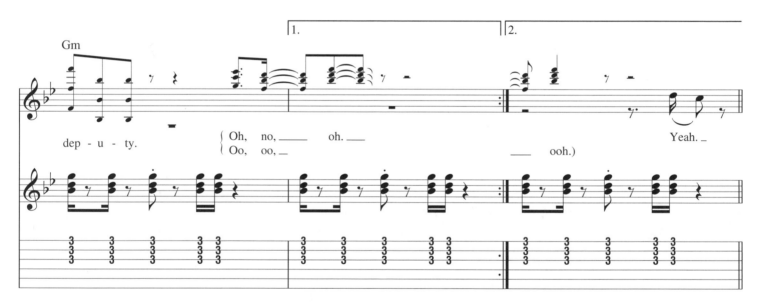

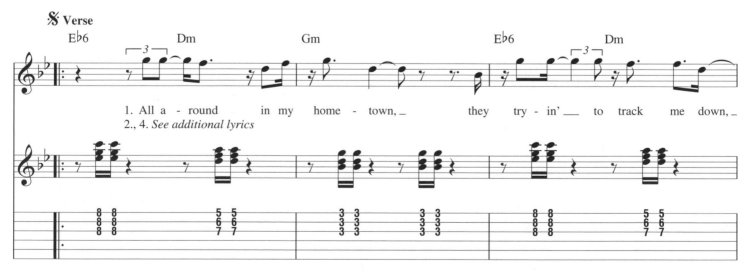

Copyright © 1974 Fifty-Six Hope Road Music Ltd. and Odnil Music Ltd.
Copyright Renewed
All Rights in North America Administered by Blue Mountain Music Ltd./Irish Town Songs (ASCAP)
and throughout the rest of the world by Blue Mountain Music Ltd. (PRS)
All Rights Reserved

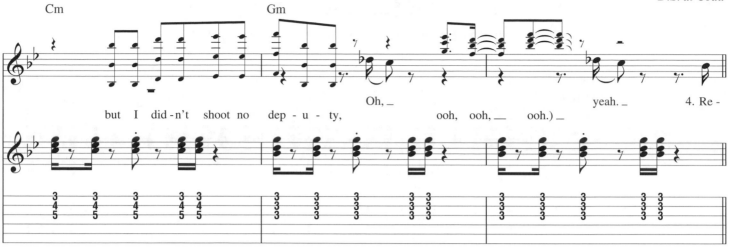

but I did-n't shoot no dep-u-ty, Oh, ___ ooh, ooh, ___ ooh.) ___ yeah. ___ 4. Re-

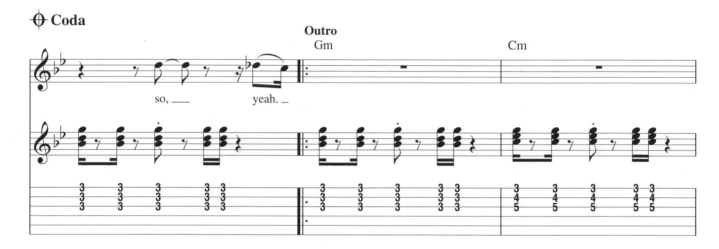

so, ___ yeah. ___

Repeat and fade

Additional Lyrics

2. Sheriff John Brown always hated me.
   For what, I don't know.
   Ev'ry time I plant a seed, he said kill it before it grows.
   He said, kill them before they grow.
   And so, and so, read it in the news.

Chorus 2. (I shot the sheriff.) Lord,
   (But I swear it was in self-defense.) Where was the deputy?
   (Oo, oo, oo.) Oo. I say,
   I shot the sheriff.
   But I swear it was in self-defense. Yeah.

4. Reflexes had the better of me.
   And what is to be, must be.
   Ev'ryday the bucket a go a well.
   One day the bottom a go drop out.
   One day the bottom a go drop out. I say:

Chorus 3. I, I, I, I shot the sheriff.
   Lord, I didn't shot the deputy. No.
   Yeah, I, I, (Shot the sheriff.)
   But I didn't shoot no deputy. Yeah.

Buffalo Soldier

Words and Music by Noel Williams and Bob Marley

© 1983 EMI LONGITUDE MUSIC and MUSIC SALES CORPORATION
All Rights Reserved   International Copyright Secured   Used by Permission

Stol - en from Af - ri - ca,   brought to A - mer - i - ca.   Said he was

fight - ing on ar - riv - al,   fight - ing for sur - viv - al.   Said he was a

buf - fa - lo sol - dier   in the war for A - mer - i - ca.   Sing- in',

why - yo - yo? Why - yi - yo - yo?   Why - yi - yo - yo - yo - yo - yo - yo?

Bridge

13

Outro-Chorus

buf - fa - lo sol - dier ... in the war for A - mer - i - ca.

Buf - fa - lo sol - dier,

dread - lock ras - ta. Fight - ing on ar - riv - al,

fight - ing for sur - viv - al.

The Harder They Come

Words and Music by Jimmy Cliff

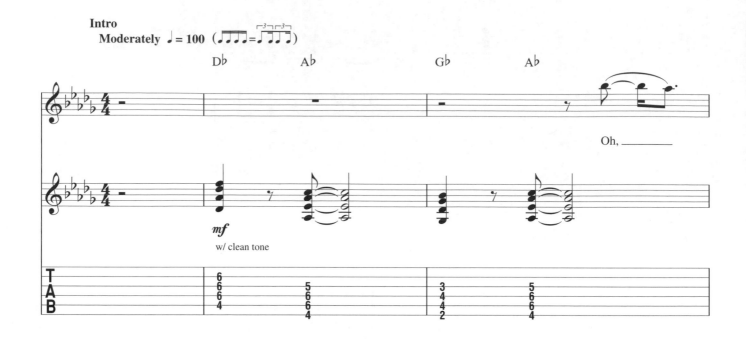

Copyright © 1972 ISLAND MUSIC LTD.
Copyright Renewed
All Rights for the United States and Canada Controlled and Administered by UNIVERSAL - SONGS OF POLYGRAM INTERNATIONAL, INC.
All Rights Reserved   Used by Permission

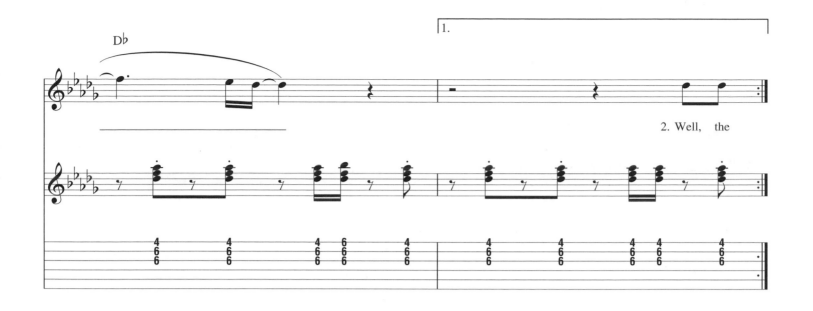

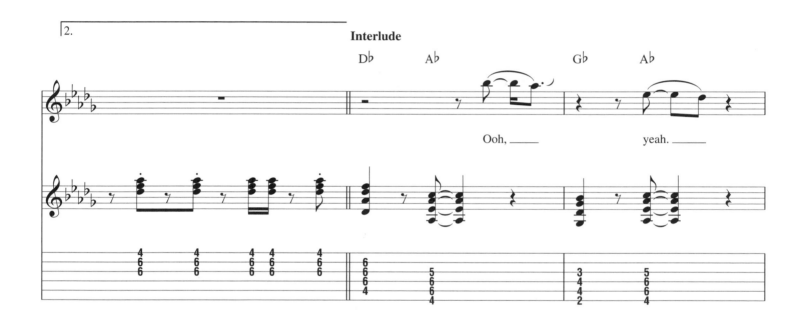

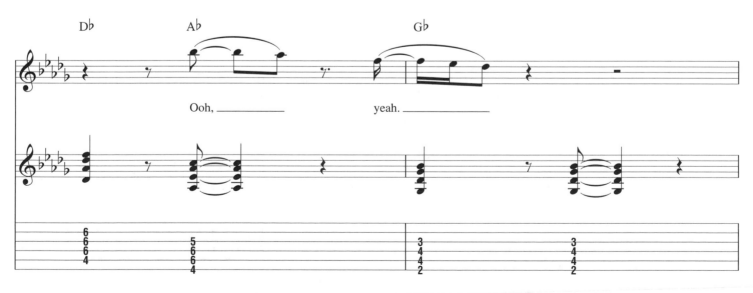

19

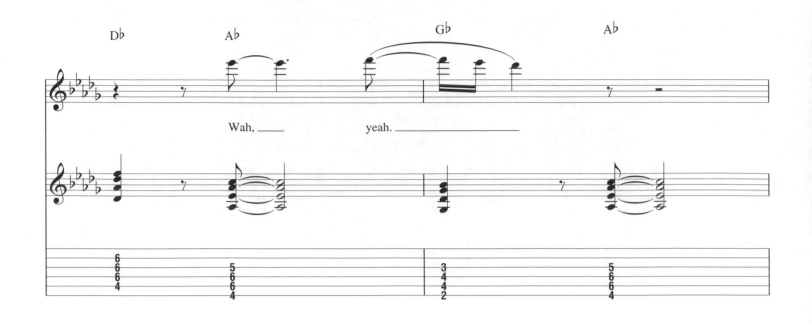

Wah, _____ yeah. _____

D.S. al Coda

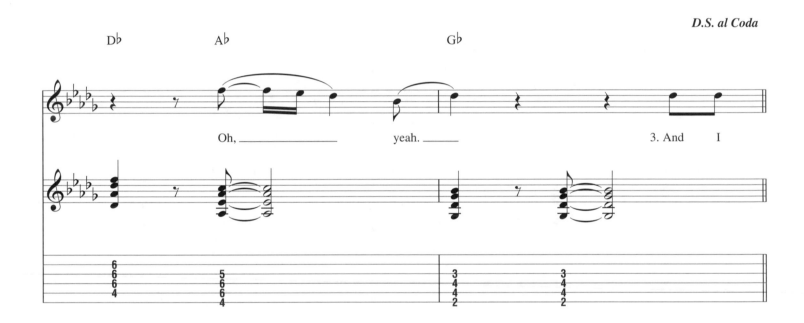

Oh, _____ yeah. _____ 3. And I

$\oplus$ **Coda**

Yeah, _ the

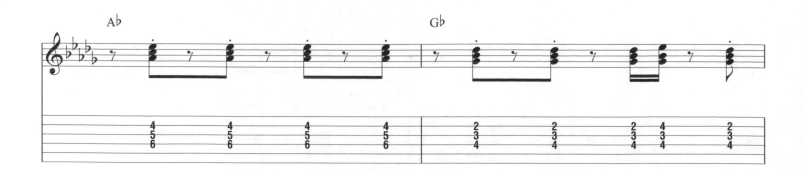

What I say ___ now, what I say, ___ one time. ___ The

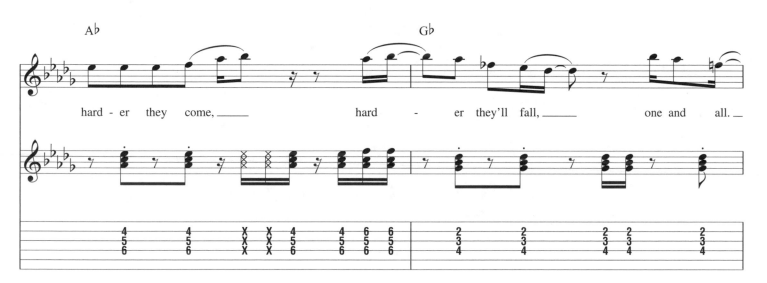

hard-er they come, ___ hard - er they'll fall, ___ one and all. ___

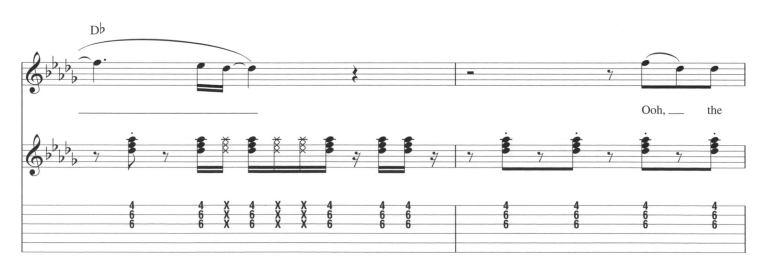

_____ Ooh, ___ the

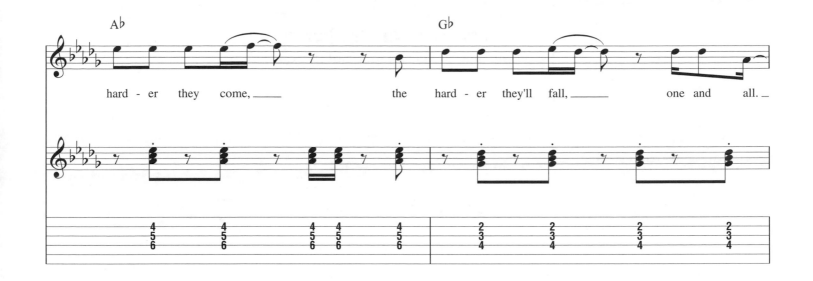

hard - er they come, _____ the hard - er they'll fall, _____ one and all. _

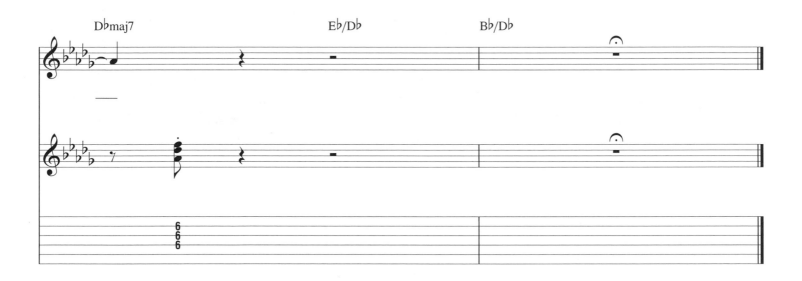

Additional Lyrics

2. Well, the oppressors are trying to keep me down,
   Trying to drive me underground.
   And they think that they have got the battle won.
   I say forgive them, Lord, they know not what they've done.
   'Cause as sure as the sun...

3. And I'll keep on fighting for the things I want,
   Though I know that when you're dead you can't.
   But I'd rather be a free man in my grave,
   Than living as a puppet or a slave.
   So as sure as the sun...

The Israelites

Words and Music by Desmond Dekker

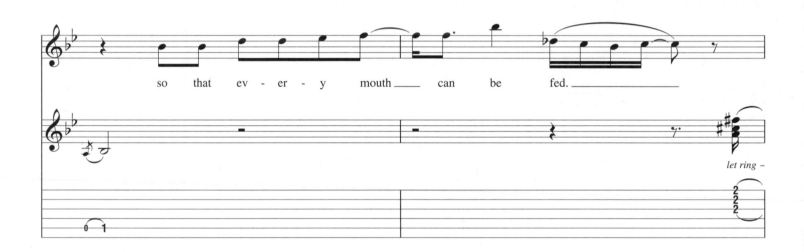

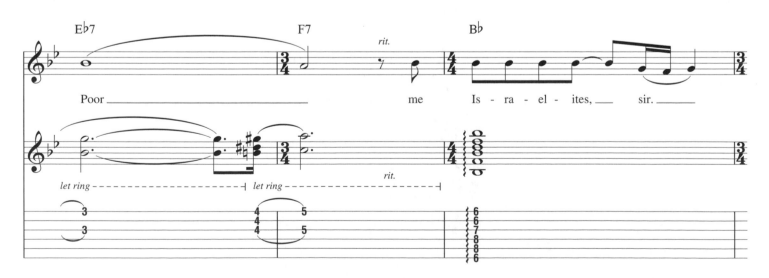

Copyright © 1969, 1975 ISLAND MUSIC LTD. and EMBASSY MUSIC CORPORATION
Copyrights Renewed
All Rights for ISLAND MUSIC LTD. in the United States and Canada Controlled and Administered by
UNIVERSAL - POLYGRAM INTERNATIONAL PUBLISHING, INC.
All Rights Reserved   Used by Permission

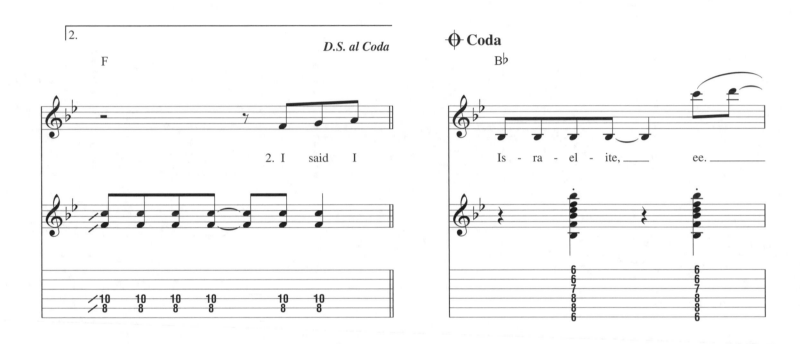

D.S. al Coda

Coda

Outro

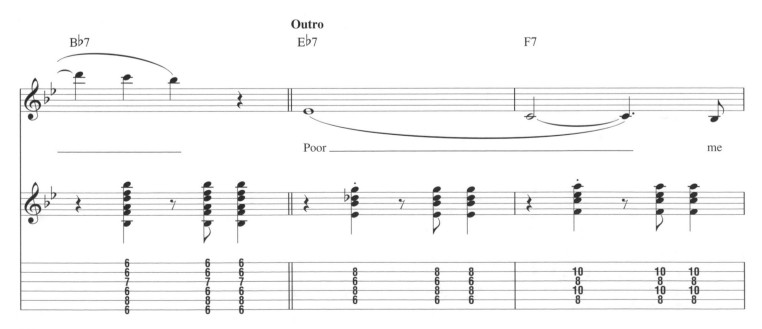

28

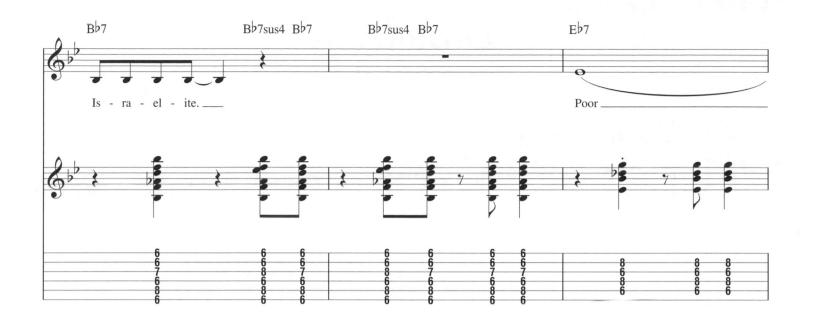

Begin fade

Fade out

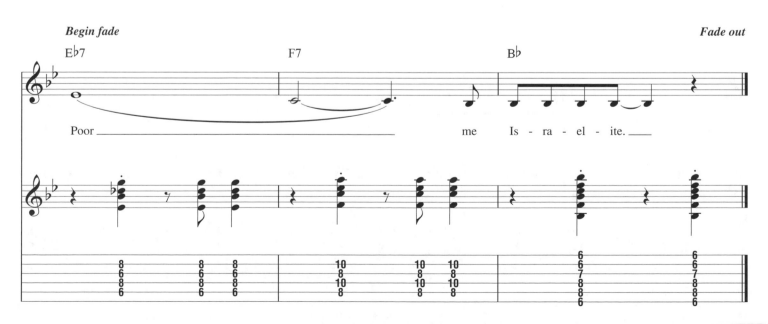

Legalize It

Words and Music by Peter Tosh

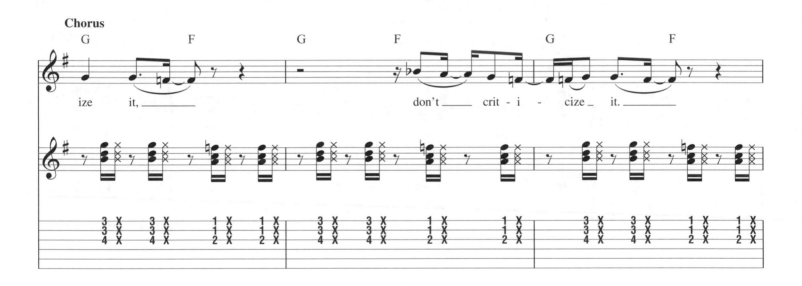

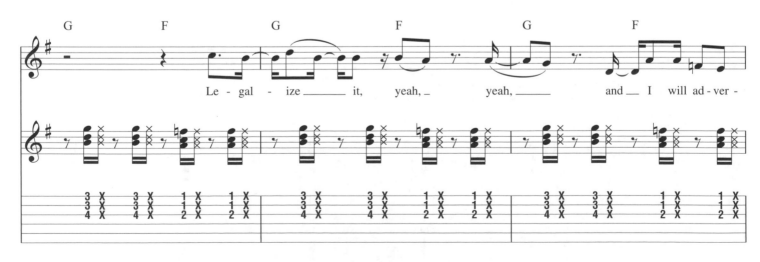

Copyright © 1975 NUMBER ELEVEN MUSIC
Copyright Renewed
All Rights Controlled and Administered by IRVING MUSIC, INC.
All Rights Reserved   Used by Permission

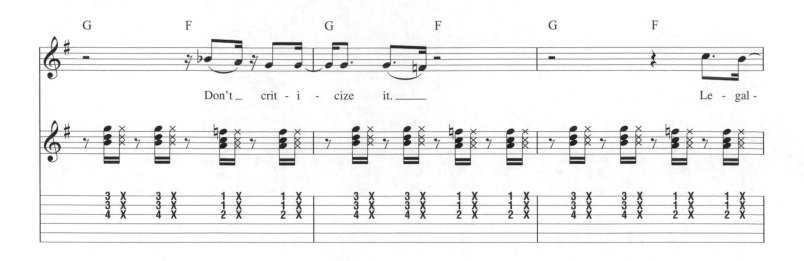

Don't __ crit - i - cize it. _____ Le - gal -

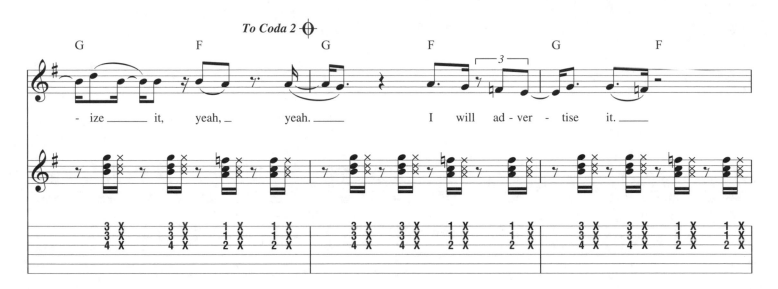

To Coda 2 ⊕

- ize _____ it, yeah, __ yeah. _____ I will ad - ver - tise it. _____

⊕ **Coda 2**

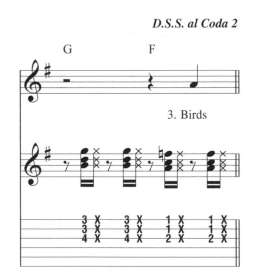

D.S.S. al Coda 2

3. Birds

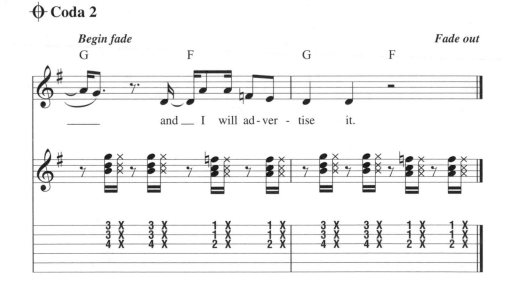

Begin fade   *Fade out*

_____ and __ I will ad - ver - tise it.

Additional Lyrics

3. Doctors smoke it, nurses smoke it.
   Judges smoke it, even the lawyer too.
   So you got to legalize it...

5. Birds eat it, ants love it.
   Fowls eat it, goats love to play with it.
   So you got to legalize it...

Marcus Garvey

Words and Music by Phillip Fullwood and Winston Rodney

Intro
Moderately slow ♩ = 92

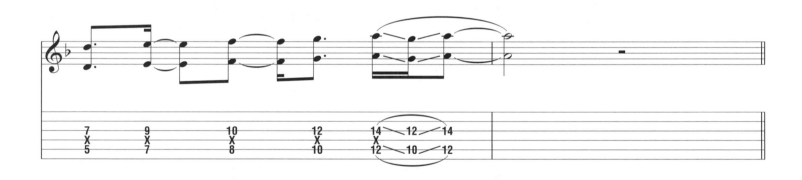

Verse

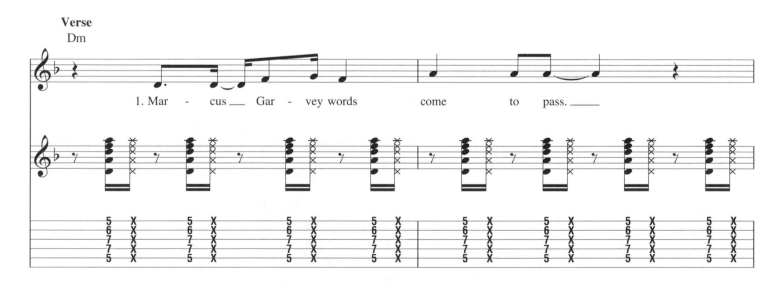

1. Mar - cus Gar - vey words come to pass. ___

Copyright © 1976 Blue Mountain Music Ltd.
Copyright Renewed
All Rights in North America Administered by Blue Mountain Music Ltd./Irish Town Songs (ASCAP)
and throughout the rest of the world by Blue Mountain Music Ltd. (PRS)
All Rights Reserved

Hel - lo. _____

Come, ev - 'ry - one, _____ come.

Chorus

Gm   Dm/F   Dm

Whoa, _____   let me do what I can.

Gm   Dm/F   Dm

Mm, _____   for you and you a - lone.

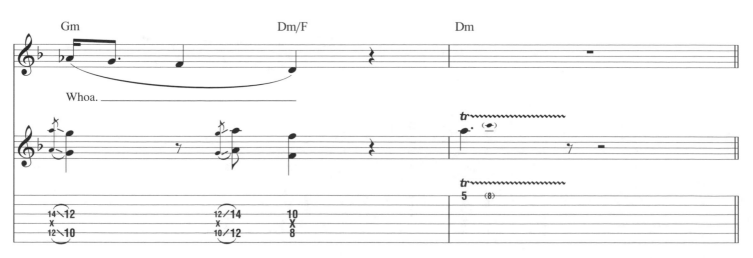

Gm   Dm/F   Dm

Whoa. _____

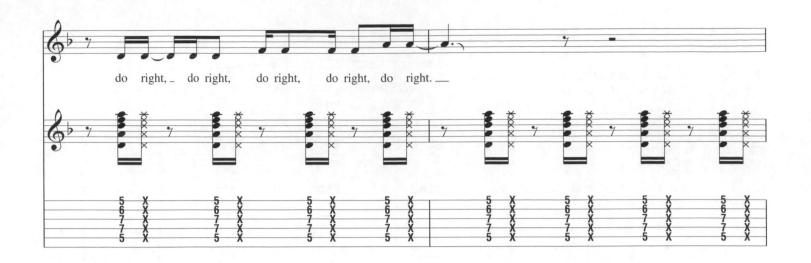

do right, _ do right, do right, do right, do right. _

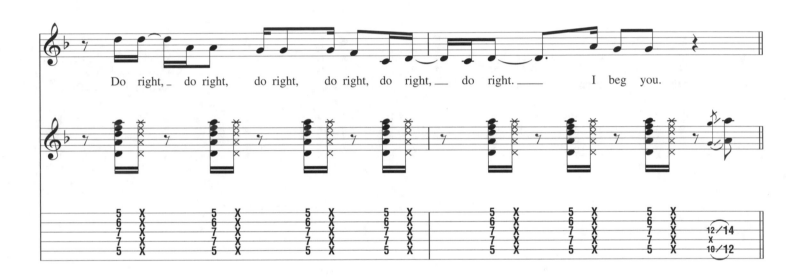

Do right, _ do right, do right, do right, do right, _ do right. _ I beg you.

Chorus

Gm   Dm/F   Dm

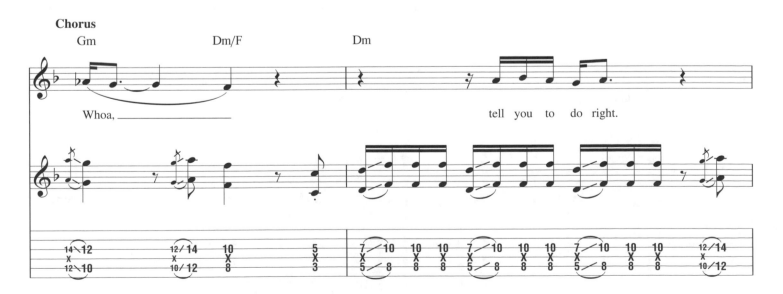

Whoa, _____ tell you to do right.

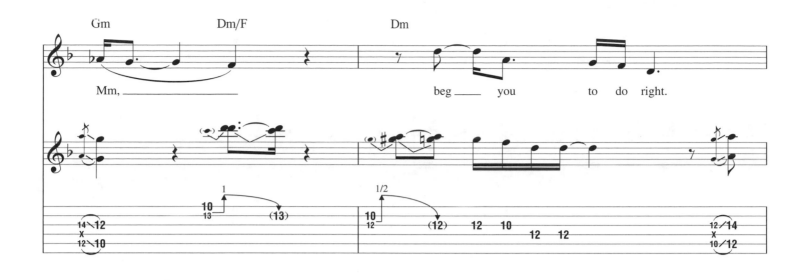

Mm, _____ beg ____ you to do right.

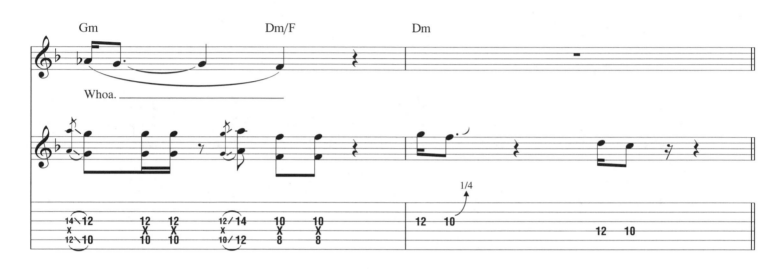

Whoa. _____

Organel Solo

Dm

Play 4 times

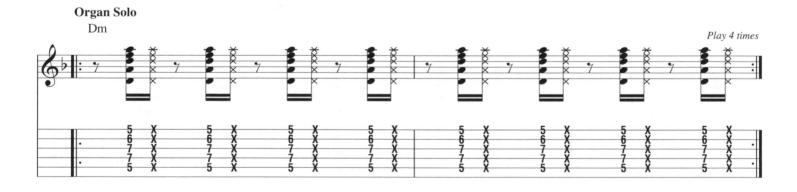

Verse

Dm

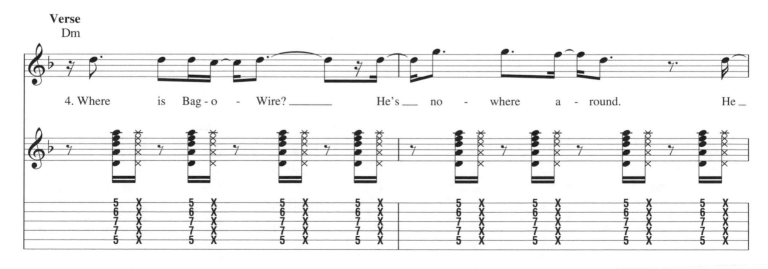

4. Where is Bag-o-Wire? _____ He's ___ no-where a-round. He ___

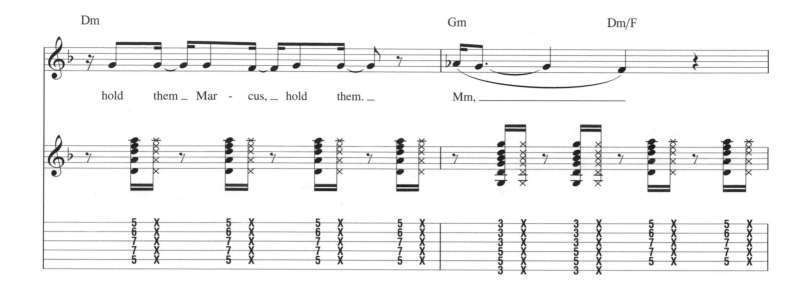

hold   them _ Mar - cus, _ hold   them. _   Mm, _____

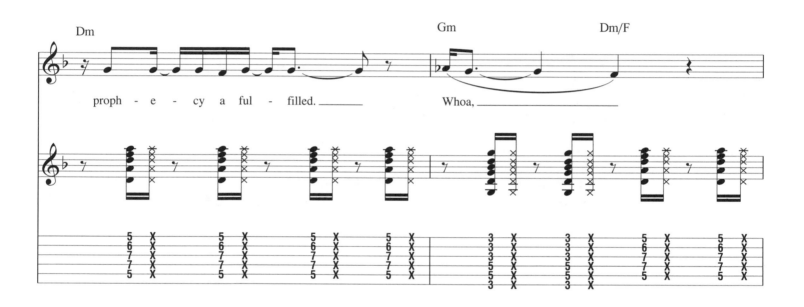

proph - e - cy a ful - filled. _____   Whoa, _____

Begin fade   *Fade out*

catch   them _ Gar - vey, _ catch   them. _   Mm. _____

Party Next Door

Words and Music by Michael Rose

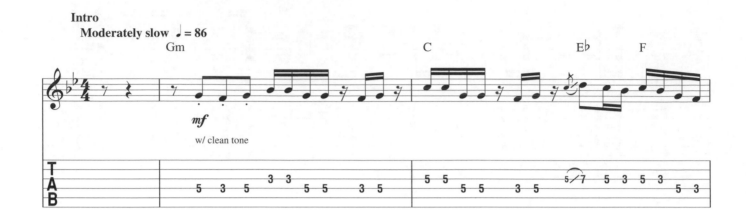

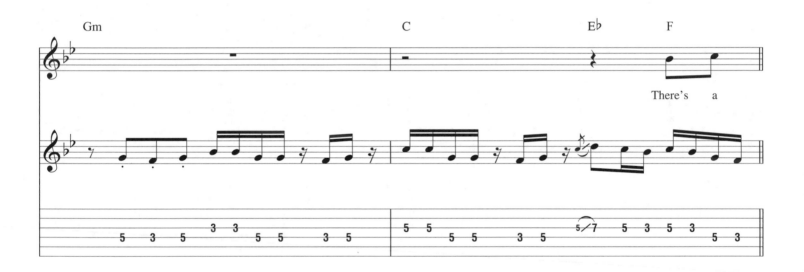

There's a

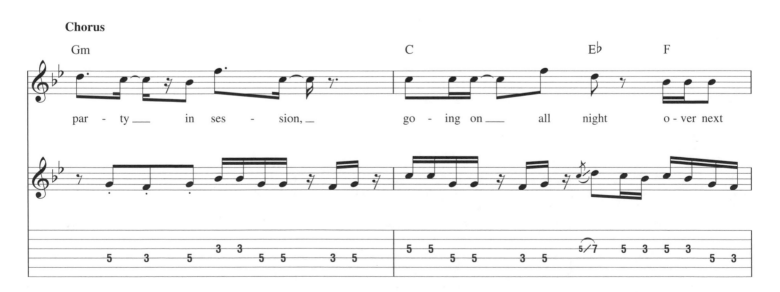

par - ty ___ in ses - sion, ___ go - ing on ___ all night o - ver next

Copyright © 1983 Rydim Music Ltd.
All Rights in North America Administered by Blue Mountain Music Ltd./Irish Town Songs (ASCAP)
and throughout the rest of the world by Blue Mountain Music Ltd. (PRS)
All Rights Reserved

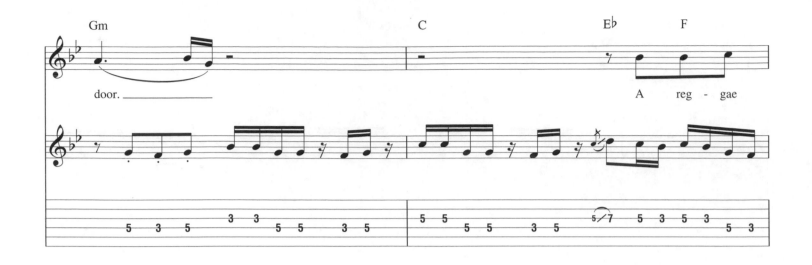

door. _____

A reg - gae

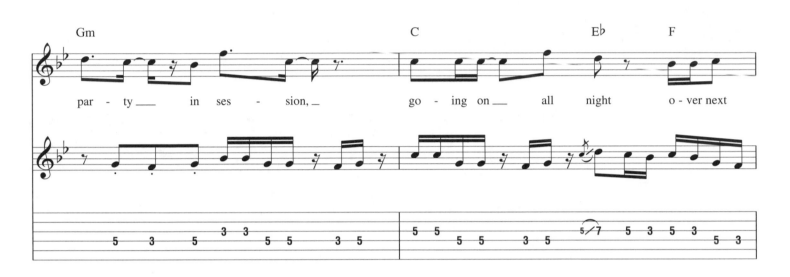

par - ty ___ in ses - sion, ___

go - ing on ___ all night o - ver next

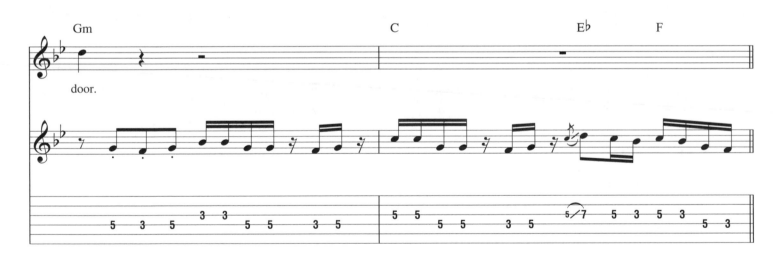

door.

Interlude

door.

Verse

1. Don't sit a-round and get ___ la - zy. Get

up, go dance ___ with a la - dy.

Pre - cious time, so a - maz - ing. ___

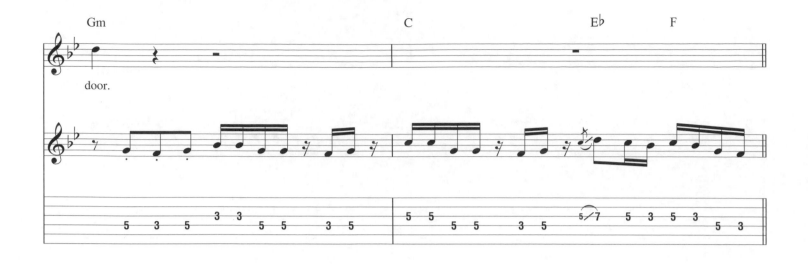

door.

Interlude

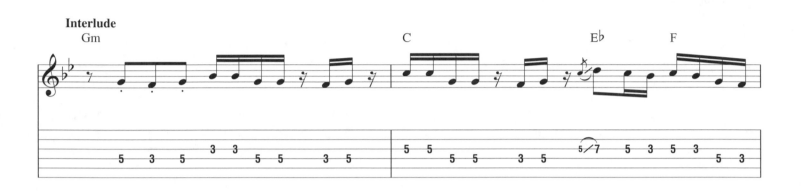

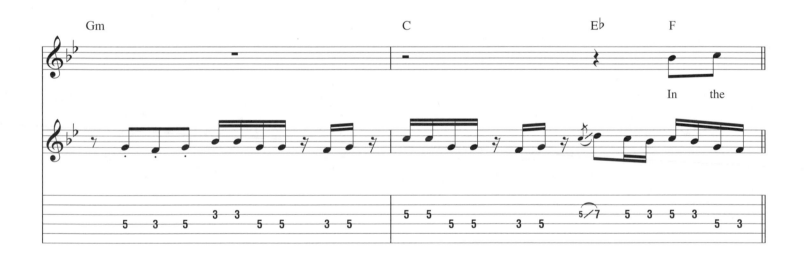

In the

Chorus

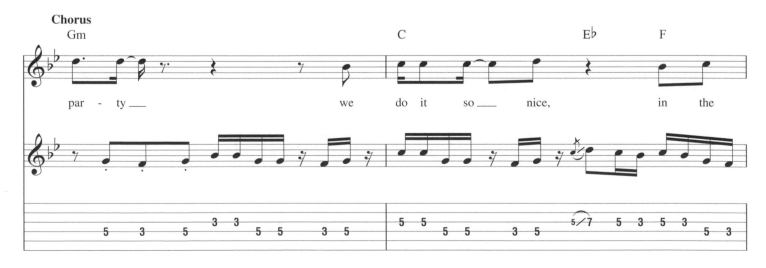

par - ty ___ we do it so ___ nice, in the

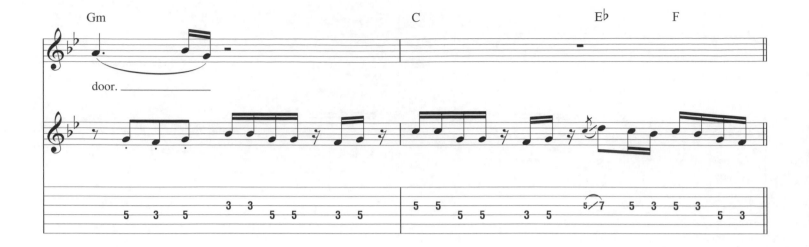

door. _____

Interlude

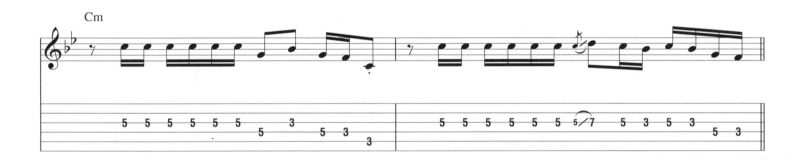

Play 4 times

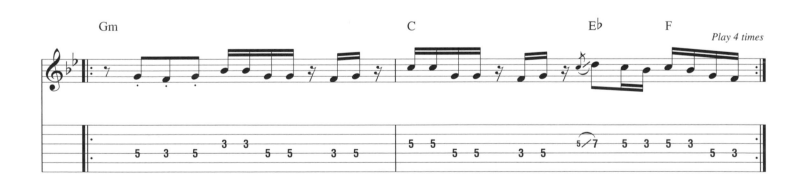

Chorus

There's a par - ty in ses - sion, _

53

Tomorrow People

Words and Music by Ziggy Marley

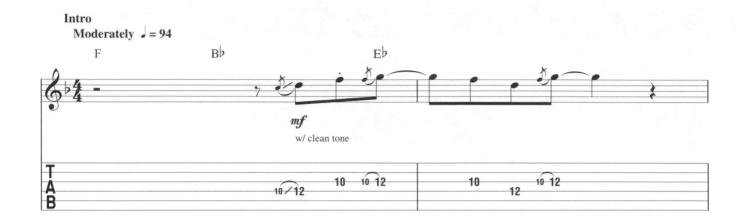

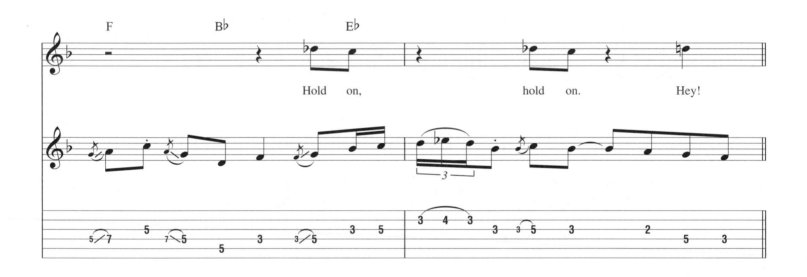

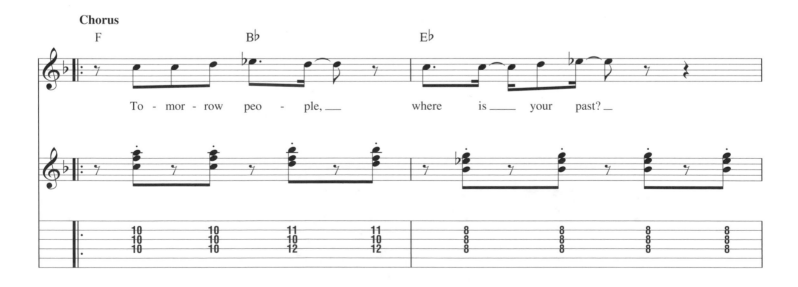

© 1988 Ishti Music
All Rights Reserved   Used by Permission

Bridge

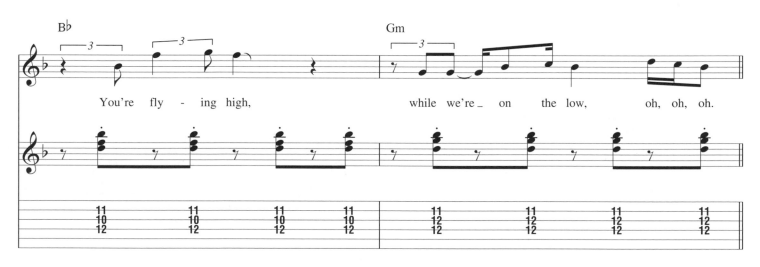

Chorus

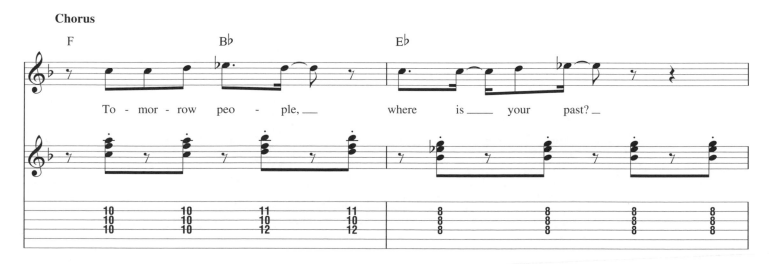

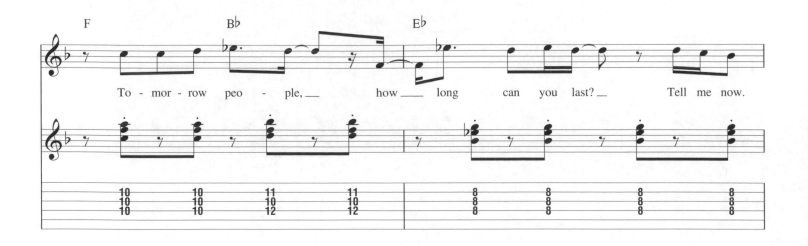

To - mor - row peo - ple, _ how _ long can you last? _ Tell me now.

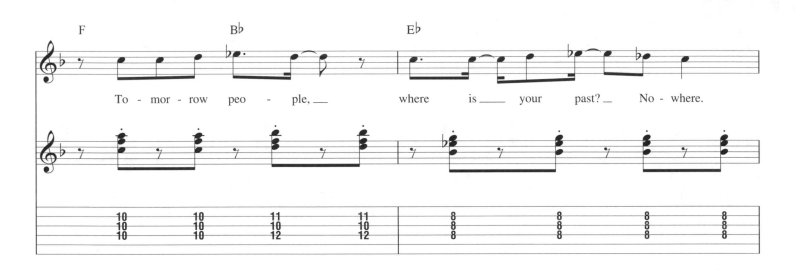

To - mor - row peo - ple, _ where is _ your past? _ No - where.

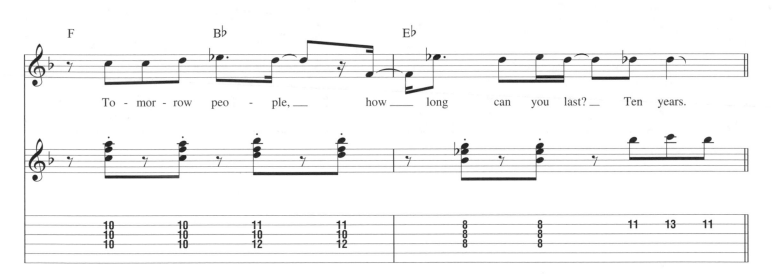

To - mor - row peo - ple, _ how _ long can you last? _ Ten years.

Guitar Solo

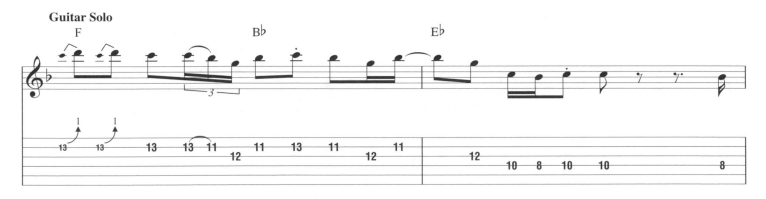

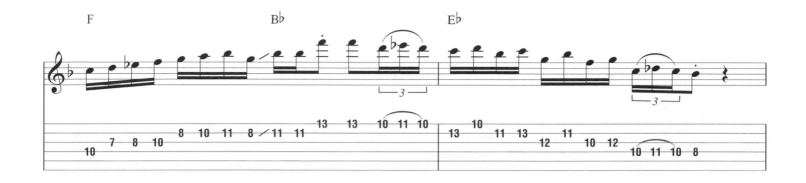

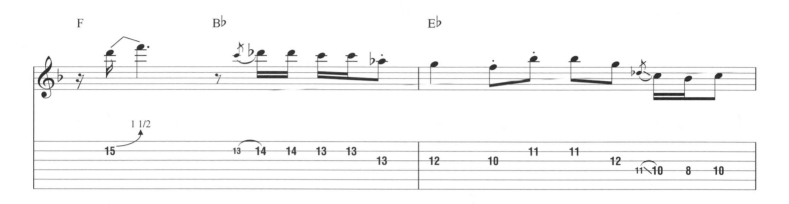

D.S. al Coda

Stop tell - in' me the same ___ stor - ies.

⊕ Coda

To - mor - row, to - mor - row peo - ple. ___ Come on. ___

Outro

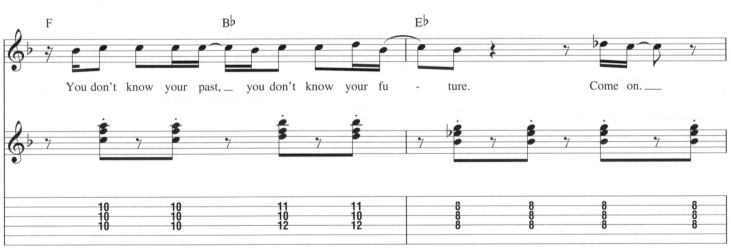

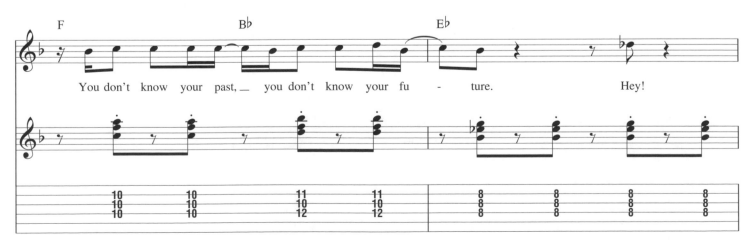

Additional Lyrics

2. Today you said you there, hey,
   Tomorrow you say you're gone
   And you're not come back.
   If there is no love in your heart, oh now,
   There will never be hope for you.

Chorus Tomorrow people, where is your past?
   Tomorrow people, how long can you last? Ten years.
   Tomorrow people, where is your past?
   Tomorrow, tomorrow people. Come on.

GUITAR PLAY-ALONG

INCLUDES TAB

This series will help you play your favorite songs quickly and easily. Just follow the tab and listen to the CD to hear how the guitar should sound, and then play along using the separate backing tracks. Mac or PC users can also slow down the tempo without changing pitch by using the CD in their computer. The melody and lyrics are included in the book so that you can sing or simply follow along.

1. ROCK
00699570...................$16.99

2. ACOUSTIC
00699569...................$16.95

3. HARD ROCK
00699573...................$16.95

4. POP/ROCK
00699571...................$16.99

5. MODERN ROCK
00699574...................$16.99

6. '90s ROCK
00699572...................$16.99

7. BLUES
00699575...................$16.95

8. ROCK
00699585...................$14.99

9. PUNK ROCK
00699576...................$14.95

10. ACOUSTIC
00699586...................$16.95

11. EARLY ROCK
0699579...................$14.95

12. POP/ROCK
00699587...................$14.95

13. FOLK ROCK
00699581...................$15.99

14. BLUES ROCK
00699582...................$16.95

15. R&B
00699583...................$14.95

16. JAZZ
00699584...................$15.95

17. COUNTRY
00699588...................$15.95

18. ACOUSTIC ROCK
00699577...................$15.95

19. SOUL
00699578...................$14.99

20. ROCKABILLY
00699580...................$14.95

21. YULETIDE
00699602...................$14.95

22. CHRISTMAS
00699600...................$15.95

23. SURF
00699635...................$14.95

24. ERIC CLAPTON
00699649...................$17.99

25. LENNON & McCARTNEY
00699642...................$16.99

26. ELVIS PRESLEY
00699643...................$14.95

27. DAVID LEE ROTH
00699645...................$16.95

28. GREG KOCH
00699646...................$14.95

29. BOB SEGER
00699647...................$15.99

30. KISS
00699644...................$16.99

31. CHRISTMAS HITS
00699652...................$14.95

32. THE OFFSPRING
00699653...................$14.95

33. ACOUSTIC CLASSICS
00699656...................$16.95

34. CLASSIC ROCK
00699658...................$16.95

35. HAIR METAL
00699660...................$16.95

36. SOUTHERN ROCK
00699661...................$16.95

37. ACOUSTIC METAL
00699662...................$16.95

38. BLUES
00699663...................$16.95

39. '80s METAL
00699664...................$16.99

40. INCUBUS
00699668...................$17.95

41. ERIC CLAPTON
00699669...................$16.95

42. 2000s ROCK
00699670...................$16.99

43. LYNYRD SKYNYRD
00699681...................$17.95

44. JAZZ
00699689...................$14.99

45. TV THEMES
00699718...................$14.95

46. MAINSTREAM ROCK
00699722...................$16.95

47. HENDRIX SMASH HITS
00699723...................$19.95

48. AEROSMITH CLASSICS
00699724...................$17.99

49. STEVIE RAY VAUGHAN
00699725...................$17.99

51. ALTERNATIVE '90s
00699727...................$14.99

52. FUNK
00699728...................$14.95

53. DISCO
00699729...................$14.99

54. HEAVY METAL
00699730...................$14.95

55. POP METAL
00699731...................$14.95

56. FOO FIGHTERS
00699749...................$15.99

57. SYSTEM OF A DOWN
00699751...................$14.95

58. BLINK-182
00699772...................$14.95

60. 3 DOORS DOWN
00699774...................$14.95

61. SLIPKNOT
00699775...................$16.99

62. CHRISTMAS CAROLS
00699798...................$12.95

63. CREEDENCE CLEARWATER REVIVAL
00699802...................$16.99

64. OZZY OSBOURNE
00699803...................$16.99

65. THE DOORS
00699806...................$16.99

66. THE ROLLING STONES
00699807...................$16.95

67. BLACK SABBATH
00699808...................$16.99

68. PINK FLOYD – DARK SIDE OF THE MOON
00699809...................$16.99

69. ACOUSTIC FAVORITES
00699810...................$14.95

70. OZZY OSBOURNE
00699805...................$16.99

71. CHRISTIAN ROCK
00699824...................$14.95

72. ACOUSTIC '90s
00699827...................$14.95

73. BLUESY ROCK
00699829...................$16.99

74. PAUL BALOCHE
00699831...................$14.95

75. TOM PETTY
00699882...................$16.99

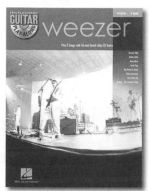  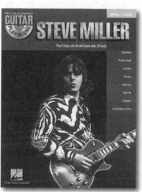  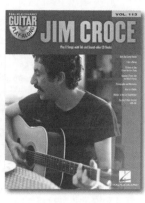

76. COUNTRY HITS
00699884..................$14.95

77. BLUEGRASS
00699910..................$14.99

78. NIRVANA
00700132..................$16.99

79. NEIL YOUNG
00700133..................$24.99

80. ACOUSTIC ANTHOLOGY
00700175..................$19.95

81. ROCK ANTHOLOGY
00700176..................$22.99

82. EASY ROCK SONGS
00700177..................$12.99

83. THREE CHORD SONGS
00700178..................$16.99

84. STEELY DAN
00700200..................$16.99

85. THE POLICE
00700269..................$16.99

86. BOSTON
00700465..................$16.99

87. ACOUSTIC WOMEN
00700763..................$14.99

88. GRUNGE
00700467..................$16.99

90. CLASSICAL POP
00700469..................$14.99

91. BLUES INSTRUMENTALS
00700505..................$14.99

92. EARLY ROCK INSTRUMENTALS
00700506..................$14.99

93. ROCK INSTRUMENTALS
00700507..................$16.99

95. BLUES CLASSICS
00700509..................$14.99

96. THIRD DAY
00700560..................$14.95

97. ROCK BAND
00700703..................$14.99

98. ROCK BAND
00700704..................$14.95

99. ZZ TOP
00700762..................$16.99

100. B.B. KING
00700466..................$16.99

101. SONGS FOR BEGINNERS
00701917..................$14.99

102. CLASSIC PUNK
00700769..................$14.99

103. SWITCHFOOT
00700773..................$16.99

104. DUANE ALLMAN
00700846..................$16.99

106. WEEZER
00700958..................$14.99

107. CREAM
00701069..................$16.99

108. THE WHO
00701053..................$16.99

109. STEVE MILLER
00701054..................$14.99

111. JOHN MELLENCAMP
00701056..................$14.99

112. QUEEN
00701052..................$16.99

113. JIM CROCE
00701058..................$15.99

114. BON JOVI
00701060..................$14.99

115. JOHNNY CASH
00701070..................$16.99

116. THE VENTURES
00701124..................$14.99

118. ERIC JOHNSON
00701353..................$14.99

119. AC/DC CLASSICS
00701356..................$17.99

120. PROGRESSIVE ROCK
00701457..................$14.99

121. U2
00701508..................$16.99

123. LENNON & MCCARTNEY ACOUSTIC
00701614..................$16.99

124. MODERN WORSHIP
00701629..................$14.99

125. JEFF BECK
00701687..................$16.99

126. BOB MARLEY
00701701..................$16.99

127. 1970s ROCK
00701739..................$14.99

128. 1960s ROCK
00701740..................$14.99

129. MEGADETH
00701741..................$16.99

131. 1990s ROCK
00701743..................$14.99

132. COUNTRY ROCK
00701757..................$15.99

133. TAYLOR SWIFT
00701894..................$16.99

134. AVENGED SEVENFOLD
00701906..................$16.99

136. GUITAR THEMES
00701922..................$14.99

138. BLUEGRASS CLASSICS
00701967..................$14.99

139. GARY MOORE
00702370..................$16.99

140. MORE STEVIE RAY VAUGHAN
00702396..................$17.99

141. ACOUSTIC HITS
00702401..................$16.99

142. KINGS OF LEON
00702418..................$16.99

144. DJANGO REINHARDT
00702531..................$16.99

145. DEF LEPPARD
00702532..................$16.99

147. SIMON & GARFUNKEL
14041591..................$16.99

149. AC/DC HITS
14041593..................$17.99

150. ZAKK WYLDE
02501717..................$16.99

153. RED HOT CHILI PEPPERS
00702990..................$19.99

157. FLEETWOOD MAC
00101382..................$16.99

158. ULTIMATE CHRISTMAS
00101889..................$14.99

161. THE EAGLES – ACOUSTIC
00102659..................$16.99

162. THE EAGLES HITS
00102667..................$17.99

166. MODERN BLUES
00700764..................$16.99

HAL•LEONARD® CORPORATION
7777 W. BLUEMOUND RD. P.O. BOX 13819 MILWAUKEE, WI 53213

For complete songlists, visit Hal Leonard online at
www.halleonard.com

Prices, contents, and availability subject to change without notice.

0113

GUITAR NOTATION LEGEND

THE MUSICAL STAFF shows pitches and rhythms and is divided by bar lines into measures. Pitches are named after the first seven letters of the alphabet.

TABLATURE graphically represents the guitar fingerboard. Each horizontal line represents a string, and each number represents a fret.

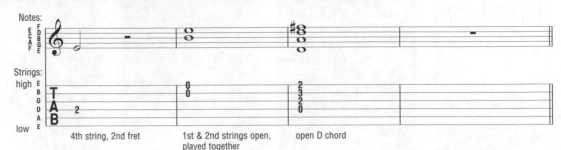

4th string, 2nd fret   1st & 2nd strings open, played together   open D chord

HALF-STEP BEND: Strike the note and bend up 1/2 step.

WHOLE-STEP BEND: Strike the note and bend up one step.

GRACE NOTE BEND: Strike the note and immediately bend up as indicated.

SLIGHT (MICROTONE) BEND: Strike the note and bend up 1/4 step.

BEND AND RELEASE: Strike the note and bend up as indicated, then release back to the original note. Only the first note is struck.

PRE-BEND: Bend the note as indicated, then strike it.

VIBRATO: The string is vibrated by rapidly bending and releasing the note with the fretting hand.

PALM MUTING: The note is partially muted by the pick hand lightly touching the string(s) just before the bridge.

HAMMER-ON: Strike the first (lower) note with one finger, then sound the higher note (on the same string) with another finger by fretting it without picking.

PULL-OFF: Place both fingers on the notes to be sounded. Strike the first note and without picking, pull the finger off to sound the second (lower) note.

LEGATO SLIDE: Strike the first note and then slide the same fret-hand finger up or down to the second note. The second note is not struck.

SHIFT SLIDE: Same as legato slide, except the second note is struck.

TRILL: Very rapidly alternate between the notes indicated by continuously hammering on and pulling off.

TAPPING: Hammer ("tap") the fret indicated with the pick-hand index or middle finger and pull off to the note fretted by the fret hand.

NATURAL HARMONIC: Strike the note while the fret-hand lightly touches the string directly over the fret indicated.

PINCH HARMONIC: The note is fretted normally and a harmonic is produced by adding the edge of the thumb or the tip of the index finger of the pick hand to the normal pick attack.

TREMOLO PICKING: The note is picked as rapidly and continuously as possible.

VIBRATO BAR DIVE AND RETURN: The pitch of the note or chord is dropped a specified number of steps (in rhythm), then returned to the original pitch.

VIBRATO BAR SCOOP: Depress the bar just before striking the note, then quickly release the bar.

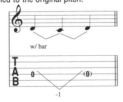

VIBRATO BAR DIP: Strike the note and then immediately drop a specified number of steps, then release back to the original pitch.

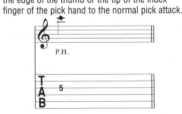

Additional Musical Definitions

 (accent) • Accentuate note (play it louder).

 (staccato) • Play the note short.

D.S. al Coda • Go back to the sign (%), then play until the measure marked "*To Coda*," then skip to the section labelled "**Coda**."

D.C. al Fine • Go back to the beginning of the song and play until the measure marked "*Fine*" (end).

Fill • Label used to identify a brief melodic figure which is to be inserted into the arrangement.

N.C. • Harmony is implied.

 • Repeat measures between signs.

• When a repeated section has different endings, play the first ending only the first time and the second ending only the second time.